CW00429295

Edi
wit

J A

Wing Commander
D E Bennett, RAF (Retd)

M H Goodall

John B Horne

Philip Morten

Adrian B Rance

ISBN 0 905280 03 2

Published by the Southampton University Industrial Archaeology Group in association with Southampton City Museums.

July 1981

Sea Planes and Flying Boats of the Solent

1

2

Many early and experimental flying boats and seaplanes were to be seen over the Solent in 1913. A marine flying base was established at Calshot in April 1913 for the Naval Wing of the Royal Flying Corps (later the Royal Naval Air Service) with Lieut. Spenser Grey RN as Flight Commander and Sub Lt. Travers RNR as flying officer. The photograph above shows how the air station had expanded by 1917. It was Winston Churchill as First Lord of the Admiralty who actively encouraged Naval Aviation. He is seen here (below) in Navy Seaplane No. 95 — a Maurice Farman aircraft — in Portsmouth Harbour. He had his first seaplane flight from Calshot on 28th August 1913. It is said that it was Churchill who coined the phrase 'seaplane' in place of the more cumbersome 'hydro-aeroplane'.

During 1910 several local enthusiasts banded together to form the Hampshire Aero Club. They established an airfield alongside Fort Grange at Gosport where they tried to fly their various machine. McArdle and Drexel started a short-lived flying school on the fringe of the New Forest at East Boldre near Beaulieu and a Southampton man, Eric Rowland Moon, established an engineering works in the medieval Wool House in Southampton: in 1910 he made a few pioneering hops in a single-seater tractor monoplane designated Moonbeam. It was powered by a 4-cylinder JAP engine but there is no evidence that it was at all successful.

These early flurries of enthusiasm produced little of significance and it was not until 1913 that the first important developments took place. In January 1913 the manager of the Cowes shipbuilding firm of John Samuel White, Edwin Carnt, formed an aircraft department. He employed Howard T Wright as the designer and the products of the partnership were designated "Wight" aircraft. The first aeroplane was a large two-seat biplane on twin floats, but on its first attempted flight, at the hands of its designer, an inexperienced pilot, it crashed and sank. However, it was rebuilt in time to be exhibited at the Olympia Aero Show held in London in March 1913. This was followed by the much more successful No.2 Navyplane which, at the hands of a pioneer test pilot Eric Gordon England, proved to have a lively performance. From the first White's saw the Royal Navy as their principal customer and the firm produced a series of two-seat float-planes intended for training and reconnaissance.

A second Solent shipbuilding firm to undertake aircraft production was S E Saunders Ltd of Cowes. The firm had a reputation for building fast single-step hydroplane motor boats using their patented Consuta system of plywood stitched with copper wire and in 1913 they undertook a joint enterprise with Sopwith Aviation Co Ltd of Kingston-on-Thames to produce a flying boat. The boat was designated Bat Boat, probably after Rudyard Kipling's futuristic vision of motor boats with wings: the hull was built by Saunders while the aircraft structure was built by Sopwith. Bat Boat was exhibited at the 1913 Olympia Aero Show and has been described as the first successful flying boat. After the show retractable wheels were fitted and H G Hawker flew it at Hamble to compete for a £500 prize offered by Mortimer Singer for a practical amphibian aircraft. On board was the Officer Commanding the newly established RNAS Station at Calshot, Lieut. Spenser Grey, who acted as official observer. The only problem was with the undercarriage which had to be lowered with a well aimed kick from Spenser Grey. The machine was purchased by Calshot where it was used extensively until the outbreak of war when it was sent to Scapa Flow. Two more Bat Boats were built: one was sold to the German Navy in 1914 while the other which was built for the Daily Mail Round Britain Race in 1914 was sold to the RNAS at Calshot.

Saunders also built beautifully finished hulls for the Wigram flying boat, the Perry-Beadle flying boat with its engine enclosed in the bows and driving twin tractor propellers by chain drive, the Bristol Coanda Biplane, the Bristol Burney Hydrofoil seaplane, the White and Thompson No.2 flying boat and the Bass-Paterson Bat Boat.

By June 1914 Sopwith had established a small works on the banks of the River Itchen at Woolston to carry on the maritime side of his aviation business. Something of the flavour of these early days is evident in the pages of Aeroplane:

"Southampton District: Very little flying was done during the past week owing to bad weather. On Thursday morning Mr Mahl was out on a Sopwith Sunbeam engined tractor and gave an acrobatic performance when starting off. He left the slipway at Woolston and was taxi-ing down the Itchen when he evidently saw something loose in the passenger seat, so instead of stopping the engine he let the machine take its course and, climbing out on the top of the fuselage, crawled along to the passenger seat, and after putting things right, crawled back, the machine continuing as if it had been under the pilot's control all the time. The seaplane had by this time travelled a good distance so it seems that Mr Mahl had confidence in its directional stability ......".

Despite the success of Bat Boat, Sopwith also developed a line of more conventional float planes and most of these were delivered to the Royal Navy. In addition one aircraft was supplied to the Greek Navy early in 1914. However, by 1916 Sopwith was building only landplanes and the Woolston buildings were incorporated into the neighbouring Supermarine works of Noel Pemberton-Billing.

Pemberton-Billing was a flamboyant and eccentric character who had already built several peculiar and unsuccessful aircraft when he arrived in Southampton in September 1913 to establish an aircraft factory at Woolston. He used the word Supermarine to describe his products and stated that his interest was to build "boats that fly rather than aeroplanes that float". He conceived the idea of a "flying lifeboat" which would fly out of the site to a ship-wreck where it would alight, shed its wings, and become an unusually stable sea-craft. His Supermarine was never built but a single seat version of the idea was exhibited at Olympia in March 1914 and this was later tested with little success on Southampton Water. The 'slip-wing' principle was used on the P.B.7 in which the aircraft could shed its wings if forced to land and proceed as a normal motor boat. Two of these were ordered by the German Government in 1914 but they were not completed and the hulls were used at Woolston as seaplane tenders. At the outbreak of war Pemberton-Billing joined the RNAS and in 1916 he resigned his commission to stand for Parliament and sold his interest in Supermarines to his partner, Hubert Scott-Paine.

The 1914 Aero Show was dominated by another Solent aircraft. This was a massive single-engined biplane of 100 ft wing span on two floats. It was designed by Fred Murphy and built as the

H.L.1 by Hamble River, Luke and Co. This company was formed in 1912 from the union of the old-established yacht builders, Luke & Co and the Hamble River Engineering Co which had built several successful racing motor boats. H.L.1 was incomplete when it was exhabited at Olympia but it is reputed to have flown afterwards. It must have been conspicuously unsuccessful for the Royal Navy failed to commandeer it in August 1914. Hamble River, Luke & Co were clearly hoping to acquire manufacturing rights of the American Curtiss flying boat but the construction of H.L.1 must have brought the company to the verge of bankruptcy. The directors showed a marked aversion to aviation after this as in December 1914 the Editor of Aeroplane was bemoaning the fact that the works of Hamble River, Luke & Co would be so useful for the repair of machines and that it was sad to see all their machinery going to waste.

Although the Solent with its long traditions of boat building was a natural place for the aircraft industry to develop in these early years, a most important impetus was provided when the Admiralty decided to establish a base for aircraft to support the fleet at Calshot. In obtaining Treasury sanction for this as one of a coastal chain of air stations, the Admiralty were clearly aware of the fact that they already owned the castle built on the spit at Calshot for Henry VIII. This could be adapted to accommodate the officers, whilst wooden sheds could be erected very cheaply to house the aircraft and the ratings. The new station was formally established on 29th March 1913 with the duties of providing aerial reconnaissance and support for the fleet, evolving new techniques of attacking the enemy with guns, bombs and torpedoes, training pilots and ground crews, and testing and accepting new aircraft from manufacturers. From the beginning the station had a space problem and took over the old coastguard cottage at Warsash to house its overflow. Additional buildings were provided there and a new pier was built on the south shore of the Hamble River in June 1914.

Two sheds were taken over from Hamble River, Luke & Co and further sheds were provided on Hamble Point. This formed the nucleus of the Marine Aircraft Acceptance Depot. Soon after the outbreak of war in 1914 the training element was moved from Calshot to Lee-on-Solent while the main station expanded into a large hutted camp around a requisitioned house at Eagle-

hurst which became linked to the hangars on the spit by a narrow-gauge railway.

The war gave a tremendous impetus to the design and manufacture of aircraft. Pemberton-Billing had to abandon most of his paper schemes but he did attract great publicity for his P.B.9 otherwise known as the 'seven-day bus'. This was a single-seat scout landplane with a 50 hp Gnome engine; it was designed, built and flown in 6 days 10 hours, although most of the components had in fact been purchased some time before at the disposal sale of a bankrupt designer. Pemberton-Billing, and after 1916, Supermarine Aviation Works Ltd. built three types of landplane and three types of marine aircraft during the war years. It was the marine aircraft that provided most of the work for the factory and which shaped its post-war fortunes.

The wartime demand for aircraft led the Admiralty to construct sheds at Hythe on Southampton Water for the construction of flying boats. These were taken over by the firm of May, Harden and May, a firm which had started as boat builders on the River Thames at Hampton Wick. M.H. & M. was taken over as part of the firm of Holt Thomas which was given the contract to build and develop the famous Porte Felixstowe flying boat. About 80 Felixstowes including 10 of the Porte/Felixstowe Baby flying boats with their giant wing-span of 124 ft and three Rolls Royce engines, were built at Hythe. May, Harden & May also built a number of AD flying boat hulls for Supermarine but the firm was eventually sold by Holt Thomas and the sheds were taken over by Supermarine about May 1927.

The war brought orders to Saunders for AVRO 504A's and Short 184's and the firm built experimental hulls for the Curtiss H4 Flying boat which gave rise to the Porte Felixstowe. Sheds were built near Folly Inn on the east bank of the Medina and an airfield was laid out near there. Later in the war they were given substantial orders for the construction of Felixstowe F2A and F5 Flying Boats as well as for Norman Thompson NT2B Flying Boat Trainers. They also built gondolas for the airships HMA 31 and HMA 32, floats and spares for other companies' aircraft and some 100,000 square feet of Consuta plywood. Vickers acquired a 50% interest in the firm towards the end of the war and Saunders built the hulls for a number of Vickers-designed flying boats including the Valentia and Viking I, II

and III. In 1928 controlling interest in the firm was acquired by A.V. Roe.

J S White's improved Navyplane was ordered in some quantity in 1914 and a few of these went to the Dardenelles on the seaplane carrier Ark Royal. After building a number of prototypes, including a large twin-fuselage torpedo bomber, White's produced their very successful Type 840 two-seat torpedo bomber/reconnaissance seaplane of which 54 were built. The firm also built a large 275 hp Rolls Royce engined bomber designed to carry eight 100 lb bombs or two 250 lb bombs but the order for 20 was cancelled when the prototype crashed and official policy changed in favour of twin engined bombers. Production in the later days of the war consisted mainly of prototypes and experimental work and the Aircraft Department of White's closed down in 1919.

Two established aircraft companies were attracted to the Solent during the First World War. In 1916 the Fairey Aviation Company of Hayes, Middlesex took over some of the buildings of the Admiralty aircraft acceptance depot at Hamble Point for the assembly and flight testing of floatplanes built at Hayes. The company continued to build aircraft including the famous Fairey IIIF until flying boats tended to overshadow the seaplane in the RAF. In 1945 the works were transferred to the associated boat building company, Fairey Marine Ltd. About one mile to the north the Avro company built a small factory in 1916. Land was purchased by A V Roe who commissioned an architect to design a purpose-built factory and a garden city suburb for his workers. In the event, wartime restrictions prevented his moving his entire workforce down from Manchester but he did move the design team down and his factory as well as some of the houses were built.

4

A VOL PLANÉ VIEW OF
THE WORKS

SUPERMARINE FACTORY

The base at Calshot gave a boost to aviation industries in the area. By the summer of 1914 two aircraft firms had established themselves on the River Itchen at Woolston. The first to arrive was Noel Pemberton-Billing who converted a coal wharf into a 'flying factory' in September 1913. He was followed in June 1914 by T O M Sopwith, with whom he shared a slipway. Sopwith No.137 of the RNAS is seen here descending the slipway at Woolston early in 1914. It was fitted with a 120 hp Austro-Daimler engine and was one of about a dozen Sopwith floatplanes supplied to the Navy before the war.

Pemberton-Billing, a great eccentric, aviation enthusiast and enterpreneur, produced a number of designs with the designation PB, known as "Supermarines".

His idea was to produce 'boats that fly rather than aeroplanes that float'. P.B.1 was a single seater bi-plane flying boat powered by a 50 hp Ghome rotary engine. It was exhibited at the 1914 Olympia Air Show but it is doubtful if it ever flew. Pemberton-Billing's assistant was Hubert Scott-Paine, later to become owner-manager of Supermarine Aviation Works Ltd.

5

6

7

The **Aeroplane** for 9th October 1913 reported:

"There has been a considerable amount of flying on the Solent recently. The Borel monoplane and Sopwith-Anzani biplane, the former piloted by Lieut Bigsworth and Sub-Lieut Travers RNR and the latter by Lieut Spenser Grey RN, both being out".

The Sopwith "Bat-Boat" (above) was built in 1912. The aircraft structure was built by Sopwith at Kingston-on-Thames and the **Consuta** plywood hull by Saunders of Cowes. It was sent to Calshot for testing where it was used extensively to develop bombing techniques and was one of the aircraft flown in by Churchill. The Borel monoplane No.83 of the RNAS is seen here (centre) in April 1913 probably at Hamble. The Admiralty ordered 8 of these seaplanes from the firm of G Borel & Cie in July 1913. They were powered by an 80 hp Gnome rotary engine and were used for training and reconnaissance. The company failed in 1914. Lieut. Travers was also passenger during test flights, piloted by Gordon England of the "Wight" Navyplane built by J S White's of Cowes to designs by Howard Wright in 1913 (below).

8   9

10

The Great War gave a great boost to aircraft design and production. The Admiralty built new sheds at Hythe for the construction of flying boats and these were taken over by May, Harden and May who built about 80 Felixstowe flying boats there. The firm also built a number of AD flying boat hulls for Supermarine. May, Harden and May were sold by their parent company, Holt Thomas, and the sheds were eventually taken over by Vickers Supermarine in the late 1920s. This photograph of the sheds (above) was taken about 1937.

Felixstowe flying boats (seen here at Hythe and in Southampton Water in 1917) were also built by another boat-building firm, Camper and Nicholson, who had established the Gosport Aviation Co Ltd.early in the war to build flying boats for the RNAS. When they received an order for Felixstowe flying boats they utilised extra space at Driver's Yard by Northam Bridge to build wings and to assemble the boats. The yard was close to their Northam yacht building yard which had been established in 1912. After the war, Camper and Nicholson converted a few Felixstowe F5's for passenger carrying, but failed to secure any orders.

With the outbreak of war Pemberton-Billing had to abandon most of his plans and concentrated on repairing aircraft flown back from Le Havre and on building aircraft mainly to government specifications. The firm built three types of marine aircraft in addition to a number of landplanes and experimental aircraft. The first was the AD Navyplane, a twin float, two-seat biplane with a single pusher engine. It was designed by the Admiralty but only one prototype — N9095 was built. It is seen here at Woolston with Scott-Paine and Sqn Comm. Seddon in 1915. Then came the successful AD flying boat again designed by the Admiralty with a hull of Linton Hope design. The second prototype — 1413 — is seen here (centre) on the slipway at Woolston in 1916. The third marine aircraft was the N1B Baby, a single seater pusher flying boat scout/fighter. The prototype — N59 — (below) was completed in 1918, but no production aircraft were ordered. The hull design was again of Linton Hope type and the aircraft had a profound effect on Supermarine's future as the Schneider Trophy winning "Sea Lion" aircraft were developed from the "Baby".

14

15

16

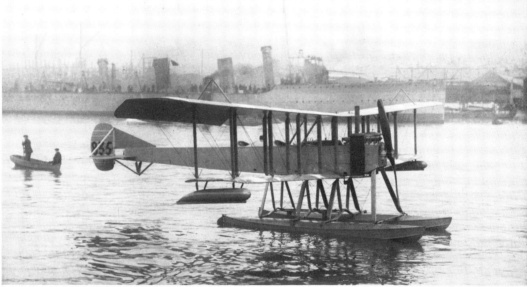

Following on the success of their Howard T Wright designed Wight Seaplane, Whites produced a number of wartime designs developing the same concept. Two trainer seaplanes were built for the RNAS and one of these, very similar to the original No 1 Seaplane, is seen here (above) on the slip at Cowes. After building a number of prototypes Whites produced their very successful Type 840 two-seat torpedo-bomber/reconnaissance seaplane fitted with a 225 hp Sunbeam engine (centre). 54 of these were built and for more than a year carried out numerous anti-submarine patrols over the Channel and North Sea. The firm's ill-fated experience with their landplane bomber led to the design being converted to a reconnaissance seaplane known as the Wight Converted Seaplane. 45 of these were built, 25 with Sunbeam Maori engines and it is one of the latter that is seen (below) at Cowes. The first submarine to be sunk by an aircraft was UB 12 sunk by a Wight Converted Seaplane on 12th August 1917.

Saunders had outstanding success with the construction of early flying boat hulls in their patent **Consuta** plywood system such as the Sopwith Bat Boat and the Perry Beadle Flying Boat of 1913 seen here (above) in Saunders shed with a BE 2 biplane in the foreground. The Perry Beadle was unsucessful and in 1915 earned the soubriquet "Jonah's Whale" on account of its tendency to stay largely submerged. During the war years a large number of flying boats were built by Saunders including Felixstowe Flying Boats. The construction of Felixstowe F2A's is seen here in Saunders works in a superb photograph of 1917. The F2A had an endurance of 6 hours, was powered by two Rolls Royce Eagle engines and was armed with up to five Lewis guns. These formidable aircraft were crucial in the U-Boat war of 1917 and it is said that one machine was actually looped by an aggrieved American trainee.

19

20

Aerial view of the Supermarine Works in 1919. The end of the Great War created a slump in the aircraft industry with no military contracts and an under-developed civil aviation industry. That Supermarine survived to become the dominant force in maritime aviation in the Solent throughout the 1920's and 1930's is largely due to the entrepreneurial flair of Hubert Scott-Paine. In 1916 Pemberton-Billing resigned his commission in the RNVR and stood for Parliament to campaign for better handling of aircraft supplies for the military. Scott-Paine became sole owner and manager of the Woolston Works and changed the name of the company to Supermarine Aviation Works Ltd. In 1919 Scott-Paine bought back most of the AD flying boats that Supermarine had built for the RNAS and converted them for civilian use as the Channel flying boat.

The first three machines to be converted were used for pleasure flying and charter work in the summer of 1919. One of them is seen here at an Isle of Wight seaside resort as it is re-fuelled. Standing in the centre is Henri Biard who joined Supermarine in 1919 as a pilot. He was selected out of 800 applicants.

The successful marketing of the Supermarine Channel managed to keep the company buoyant until military contracts were again available. Channel N1529 (later G-EAED) was used on the first international flying boat service that ran from Southampton to Le Havre during a railway strike in September 1919. The cost of the trip was £25 and it was very uncomfortable for the passengers. They certainly had their money's worth though as the trip could take up to 5 hours against headwinds. Biard recalls how one passenger brought out an umbrella! From his position behind the passenger Biard saw the danger to the propellor if the umbrella was put up and he hit the passenger on the head!

Supermarine joined with A V Roe and Beardmore Aero Engines in starting up the Bermuda and West Atlantic Air Services Ltd and two Channels were sent out to Bermuda for charter and survey work. One is seen here on a rough and ready slipway at Trinidad. A number of foreign governments bought Channel aircraft including Chile which bought some as Naval Training flying boats. One of these is seen here at the Woolston Works fitted with a machine gun in the forward cockpit and bomb dropping gear on the lower main planes.

Developing a design started in 1919 for an amphibious flying boat, Supermarine produced a prototype 'commercial amphibian' in 1920. It was a development of the Channel and was powered by a Rolls Royce Eagle VIII engine mounted as a pusher. The prototype was registered as G-EAVE and was entered for the Air Ministry Amphibian Competition held at Martlesham and Felixstowe in September 1920. The competition was won by the Vickers Viking III but in view of the Supermarine boat's outstand-ing performance the original second prize of £4,000 was doubled to £8,000. The design was developed to produce a deck-landing amphibian designated "Seal II". It was the first Supermarine flying boat with a tractor engine as seen in the prototype N146 afloat by the slipway at Woolston with its wheels raised.

The production version of the Seal II was known as the Seagull. It was fitted with a Napier Lion engine and the hull underwent several modifications. The hull construction can be seen in this photograph of a Seagull being built in March 1922. One of 22 produced for the RAF (N9605) is photographed on the slip at Woolston with the floating bridges in the background. Some of these served with the aircraft carrier HMS **Eagle** in the Mediterranean but they did not prove popular and were relegated to shore duties in 1928.

In 1925 six were bought by the Australian government to replace the RAAF's Fairy III D floatplanes. They served until 1935 when they were replaced by the Seagull MkV — better known as the Supermarine Walrus.

28

In 1923 Hubert Scott-Paine sold his interest in Supermarine to his co-director, Sqn Comm. James Bird who had joined the firm in 1919. By this time R J Mitchell, who had joined Scott-Paine in 1916, was chief designer. His first design had been the commercial amphibian of 1920, followed by the Sea Eagle produced in 1923 for the Channel Island service. Following these successes, Mitchell designed a twin-engined commercial amphibian to an Air Ministry specification. It was powered by two Rolls-Royce Eagle IX engines (later changed to Napier Lions) and was designated the Supermarine Swan. Its first flight was in March 1924 and as a result of trials carried out at the Marine Aircraft Experimental Establishment at Felixstowe a new Air Ministry specification was issued that resulted in the outstanding Supermarine Southampton. The Swan was lent to Imperial Airways in 1926 and was scrapped in 1927. Its imposing size (wing span: 69 ft) is evident in this photograph taken on the occasion of a visit to the factory by the Prince of Wales in 1924.

29

A very well known photograph of two Southamptons of No. 201 Squadron, Calshot, flying over Cowes. In only 7½ months the prototype (N218) was built and tested and Supermarine had a production order on their books. These flying boats appeared in 1925 and were not replaced until 1936. In the annals of the Royal Air Force they will always be remembered for the Far East Flight which on 14th October 1927, left on a 27,000 mile flight to Australia and Hong Kong via Singapore.

Four Southamptons led by Gp Capt. Cave-Brown-Cave undertook the flight and subsequently formed No. 205 Squadron at Singapore. The Southamptons were powered with two Napier Lion engines of 370 hp and had a maximum speed of 108 mph. The endurance was 9 hours at 83 mph or 11 hours with overload tanks.

About 20 Southamptons were built with wooden hulls, but subsequent machines were built with a lighter duralumin hull. The photograph shows a wooden Mk I in the distance with a metal Mk II in the foreground. Photographed outside the Supermarine Works (below) is the Supermarine Nanok. This was a special three engined version of the Southampton built as a torpedo-bomber for the Danish Navy. It was not accepted in this role, probably due to its lack of manoeuverability, but Supermarine managed to sell it to the Hon A E Guinness for use as an air yacht. It was fitted with a luxurious interior and became known as the Solent.

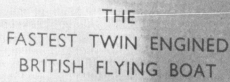

THE
FASTEST TWIN ENGINED
BRITISH FLYING BOAT
(PEGASUS ENGINES)
"CLIMBS ON ONE ENGINE WITH
FULL LOAD."

SUPERMARINE

THE SUPERMARINE AVIATION WORKS (VICKERS) LIMITED, SOUTHAMPTON, ENGLAND.

Advertisement for Supermarine. June 1935.

33

Metal construction pioneered with the Southampton was taken a step further by the introduction of metal wings on the twin-engined Seamew, an experimental amphibian designed for passenger or freight carrying. The prototype is seen here on the River Itchen with a timber ship unloading into barges at the Itchen wharves in the background. In 1931 Supermarine ·offered to build a new 'cleaned-up' version of the Southampton powered with 2 Rolls Royce Kestrel engines. It was an all metal single-bay biplane with an enclosed cockpit and went into production as the Scapa. The prototype flew in 1932 and was used to re-equip 202 Squadron based in Malta. The photograph shows some of the 13 production aircraft built for the RAF.

37

38

The Walrus amphibian originated in a requirement of the Royal Australian Air Force for a spotter flying-boat to replace the ageing Seagull III's. A prototype known as Seagull V was produced in 1934 as a private venture by Supermarine and the initial production for the RAAF was under that name. The Royal Navy having originally decided that they had no requirement for such an aircraft ordered the type as the Walrus. Its unofficial designation by those who flew it was the "Shagbat". The design had origins in the Sea King/Sea Lion aircraft developed by Mitchell out of the 1919 Baby. Large numbers of the Walrus were produced both by Supermarine and Saunders-Roe of Cowes. One is now preserved at the RAF Museum, Hendon, and one at the Fleet Air Arm Museum, Yeovilton.

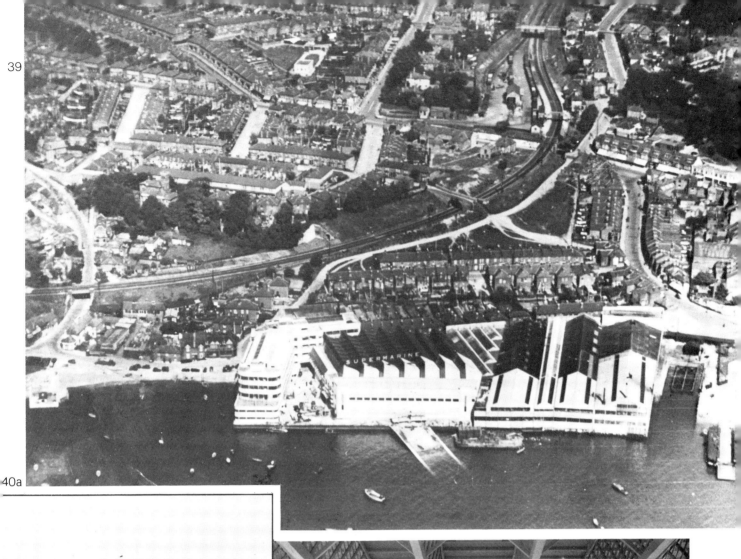

39

40a

The aerial view of the Woolston Works shows how the factory had developed by the early 1930's. Supermarine was absorbed into the Vickers group in 1928 and expansion of production soon led the company to purchase the old May, Harden & May sheds at Hythe and, in the later 1930's, to build a new works on the River Itchen, upstream of the Woolston Works. The Woolston Works were destroyed by enemy action in 1940 and was never occupied by the company.

The last of the long line of biplane flying boats designed by R J Mitchell was the Stranraer. It was, like the Scapa, based on the successful Southampton and with its all metal construction and twin Bristol Pegasus engines had a performance superior to any contemporary — civil or military. The first Stranraers entered service in 1936 with No. 228 Squadron at Pembroke Dock and remained in service until replaced by Short

Sunderlands in 1940. A number were also built for the Canadian Air Force by Canadian Vickers, and one of these is on display at the RAF Museum, Hendon.

40

A common and, no doubt, popular, sight in the Solent area during the late 1920's and 1930's were the Fairey IIIF seaplanes of the Fleet Air Arm. These aircraft, fitted with a 450 hp Napier Lion water-cooled engine were introduced in 1927 and had a successful career with both the RAF and the Fleet Air Arm as a landplane and a seaplane. The photograph (above) shows the Fairey IIIF S1520 attracting the crowds at Ventnor, Isle of Wight about 1933. It was probably from the School of Naval Co-Operation at Lee-on-the-Solent. A training station for seaplane pilots was established there in July 1917 by the Royal Naval Air Service: originally a crane was used to lift the aircraft into the water but in 1918 three slipways were built. An aero-drome was built behind the seaplane station in 1937 and enlarged during the Second World War; it is still in use as a base of the Fleet Air Arm.

The lower photograph shows a Fairey IIIF from the Seaplane Training Flight at Calshot about 1935. Fairey Aviation Co Ltd was founded by C R Fairey in 1917. The firm's association with the Solent began when it took over some Admiralty buildings at Hamble Point in 1916 for assembly and testing of floatplanes built at the main factory at Hayes, Middlesex. The first Fairey III was built in 1917 and went on to end its days as the Seal around 1940. It was also used in one form as a radio-autopilot controlled sea-plane known as the **Queen Bee**.

42

The Schneider Trophy

A magnificent trophy of silver and bronze mounted on a base of dark veined marble. A naked figure representing speed is shown swooping down to kiss a triton rising on the crest of a wave. In the breaking wave are also the heads of two other zephyrs and Neptune, God of the Sea. The trophy was an international prize offered by the French industrialist Jacques Schneider in 1913 to promote the developments of air travel by aeroplanes that could land and take off from water. By the time that Britain finally won the trophy outright in September 1931 Jacques Schneider's original quest for safe air travel had given place to a quest for speed but the genius and technological progress that this inspired was to save democracy in the summer of 1940.

Progress can be seen at least in terms of speed as over a mere 18 years the winners speed climbed from 60 mph to over 340 mph. The first contest in 1913 at Monaco was the only time that the French won the trophy using a Deperdussin hydro-aeroplane, as sea planes were then known. Britain won the trophy in 1914 and then the Great War turned attention to the military aspects of aircraft design. The war years saw great development particularly in aero-engines. In two consecutive contests after the war Italy won the trophy and a third win, according to the rules of the contest, would have meant that the trophy was permanently held by that country. Fortunately great sportsmanship by Hubert Scott-Paine of Supermarine, attention to detail by his designer R J Mitchell, the sponsorship of Napiers and the flying genius of H C Biard won the Trophy for Britain in 1922.

1923 saw the Americans introduce new design concepts and with a well organised military team at the contest held at Cowes, Isle of Wight, they were able to take the trophy across the Atlantic. Winning again in 1925 they seemed set to retain the trophy outright but the following year a remarkable effort by the Italian firms of Macchi and Fiat produced the M39 that beat the apparently invincible Americans and took the trophy back to Italy.

43

The Schneider Trophy photographed at the Royal Aero Club after the win of 1922. On the right is Hubert Scott-Paine of Supermarine, on the far left is the pilot of the Sea Lion flying boat, Captain H C Biard, and in the centre is H T Vane, managing director of Napier's whose engine powered the winning aircraft.

It was, however, a great British victory at Venice in 1927 with an R J Mitchell designed S5 that brought the contest to the Solent in 1929 for the first time in six years. In a fantastic race watched by millions, a Supermarine S6 with a special Rolls Royce engine achieved a second victory. It is perhaps typically British that the government decided not to fund further developments to ensure a third and final win for Britain in 1931, but at the last minute Lady Houston put forward £100,000 and, working against the clock, Supermarine and Rolls Royce produced the S6B aircraft that not only won the trophy but established a new world air speed record.

The Schneider Trophy, more than anything, epitomises progress in aviation and personal courage in an era when such things were of great national prestige. Governments, industry and individuals worked together to win a trophy in a spirit of competition that itself is a thing of the past. September 1981 will be the 50th anniversary of the third win by Britain: it will be an occasion for nostalgia even though the country is again in recession and even though we think nothing of flying at over 1,000 mph.

44

45

The first British win of the Schneider Trophy was at Mocaco in 1914 in a Sopwith Tabloid, a two-seater biplane piloted by Howard Pixton. A special version of the float plane was prepared and dubbed the Sopwith Schneider. It was powered by a 100 hp Gnome Monosoupage engine but when trials were carried out on the Hamble River in March 1914 it cartwheeled and sank. In the event the machine won the contest at a speed of 86.78 mph. Production versions of the Schneider single-seat scout were sup-plied for the RNAS (above) and later versions were usually known as the Sopwith Baby. These were also built by Fairey Aviation as the Hamble Baby. For the 1919 Schneider Trophy competition, Sopwith built a new machine powered by a 450 hp Cosmos Mercury engine. It is seen here being prepared for the race together with the Italian Savoia flying boat in the hangar at Saunders Works, Cowes.

47a

In 1918 Supermarine produced a single-seat fighter scout called the Supermarine Baby. After the armistice this was converted into a civilian sporting amphibian known as Sea King I. It is seen here (above) at the Woolston Works. The Royal Aero Club was given the task of organising the 1919 Schneider contest. Bournemouth was chosen as the venue and Supermarine entered a specially built racing flying boat, designed by R J Mitchell which was similar to the Sea King. Registered as G-EALP the **Sea Lion** was successful in its tests and Sqn Ldr. Hobbs was chosen as the pilot. The aircraft was powered by the newly developed 450 hp Napier Lion engine. The back up British Team comprised a Sopwith 'Schneider' seaplane, a special Avro seaplane and a Fairey IIIA. The event was badly organised and disaster struck when sea mists covered the area on 10th September, the day of the race. Hobbs had to alight in Swanage Bay to get his bearings and he damaged the hull on a floating object as he took off again. When he later landed near Boscombe the aircraft up-ended and sank (below). The contest was awarded to the Italians.

47

The decision to challenge the Italians for the Schneider Trophy in 1922 was one of the great pieces of sportsmanship for which Scott-Paine has rarely been given credit. If Britain had not won then the Italians would have taken the trophy outright and the great Supermarine S6 may never have come into being. The Supermarine entry was a specially prepared version of the production aircraft Sea King II. She was fitted with a 450 hp Lion engine provided by Napier's and the wings were slightly modified. Named **Sea Lion II**

(G-EBAH) she was piloted by Capt. H. C Biard whose clever tactics enabled Britain to snatch the trophy back from the Italian Passeleva flying an undoubtedly superior Savoia S51 flying boat. The race was won by a margin of 2 mins. 2½ secs. at a speed of 145.7 mph.

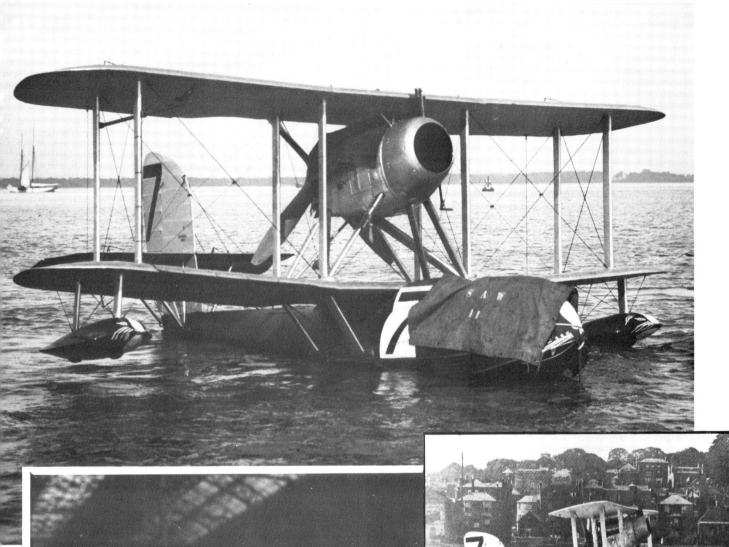

50

51a

51

Capt. Henri Biard is greeted at Victoria Station on his return from Naples by Mrs R Scott-Paine (HS-P's mother). On the right is Harold Perrin and Frederick Handley Page. Hubert Scott-Paine is behind his mother and under the ostrich feather is Mrs James Bird, wife of Scott-Paine's co-director of Supermarine. The smaller lady is Scott-Paine's sister, Katie, and under the bowler hat on the left is a member of the Royal Aero Club.

The 1923 contest was held at Cowes and Supermarine again entered with G-EBAH but somewhat modified and re-named **Sea Lion III**. The wing span was reduced by 8 ft the hull was modified as was the tail plane. The output of the Napier Lion engine was boosted to 525 hp and it was confidently expected that she would reach 160 mph. In the event **Sea Lion III** with Capt. H C Biard at the controls lapped 157.77 mph and was utterly out-classed by the American Curtiss seaplanes. The winner was a Curtiss CR-3 piloted by Lt. David Rittenhouse at a speed of 177.38 mph. American technology and American government money took the trophy to America. However, the American advances did not go un-noticed by Supermarine's R J Mitchell.

52

53

R J Mitchell's S4 (above) was introduced to the public on 25th August 1925 when it flew for the first time. The small monoplane with cantilever wings was perhaps the most elegant of all Mitchell's designs. It was totally free from bracing wires that caused so much drag — a feature, however, that probably led to its crashing at Baltimore in October of that year. The S4 was powered by a Napier Lion engine of 680 ph and again H C Biard was the pilot. Biard was lucky to escape with his life when the S4 plunged into Chesapeake Bay and the contest was won by Lieut. James Doolittle in an American Curtiss R3C-2 at a speed of 232.573 mph.

Mitchell again brought victory to Supermarine at the Schneider Trophy contest at Venice in 1927. He is seen here with the second S5 (N220) together with the team that created the aircraft and with Flt Lt. S N Webster AFC of the RAF High Speed Flight, who was the pilot.

Three Supermarine S5's were produced for the 1927 contest at Venice. Another great advance was the formation of the RAF High Speed Flight to participate in the contest for Britain. Pictured above is N220 at the RAF station, Calshot, and below is the same aircraft being wheeled out of the hangar at Woolston. Following practice flights at Calshot the aircraft were shipped to Venice on board HMS Eagle together with the Gloster racing machines. The contest was won by the S5 (N220) piloted by Flt Lt. Webster at an average speed of 281.65 mph. This was a new speed record for seaplanes.

56

The RAF High Speed Flight in 1929. After the death of Flt Lt. Sam Kinkead, Flt Lt. D'Arcy Greig (below right) joined the flight and set up a new British record of 319 mph. He was part of the team which won the trophy for the second consecutive time in 1929. The contest was won by a Supermarine S6 piloted by Flt Lt. H R D Waghorn shown here (below left) as he is carried ashore by an airman. Flg Off. R L R Atcherley (extreme right above) made a world speed record of 332 mph in N248. Sqn Ldr. Orlebar (third from right) established a record of 357.6 in N247 and Flt Lt. G Stainforth (second from right) established a record of 407.8 mph in the S6B, S1596 in 1931. Second from the left is Flg Off. T H Moon, the engineer.

57

58

The 1929 High Speed Flight had the S5, N219 for the Schneider contest of that year and two new S6 aircraft. The contest was over a four sided course starting opposite Ryde Pier. The turning points were marked by pylons mounted on destroyers. N219 flown by Flt Lt. D'Arcy Greig is seen (above) turning above one of the pylons in the race in which he took third place. Atcherley in his S6 N248 was less fortunate since he turned no more than a wing span inside one of the pylons and was disqualified. He was of course un-aware of this and continued to log the best lap of the whole series at 332 mph, breaking the world record over 50 and 100 kilometres. The S5, N220 is seen (below) on the slip at Calshot with the United States liner Leviathan in the background on its way up Southampton Water. N220 was used as a training aircraft for the flight in 1929.

For the 1929 contest Supermarine produced a development of the S5 — the S6 designed around the new Rolls Royce 'R' engine capable of developing 1,900 hp. The first S6 was N247 seen above being launched for the first time at Woolston. She was delivered to the High Speed Flight on 5th August when a number of problems became evident and she did not take off until 5 days later. Additional cooling arrangements were made as the engine overheated and eventually N247 retained the trophy averaging 328.63 mph over eight laps. The pilot, Flt Lt. H R D Waghorn was awarded the Air Force Cross. N247 was lost in practice prior to the 1931 race, flown by the only naval pilot to have served in the RAF High Speed Flight, Lt. Jerry Brinton, RN.

N247 is seen (below) from beneath while doing a tight turn during the 1929 contest. The starboard float is longer and contained more fuel than the port float. Her sister N248, now preserved in the Mitchell Memorial Museum, almost sank during the mooring trials as the float developed a leak. The contest had moved far from Jacques Schneider's original ideals.

62

Advertisement for Supermarine soon after Sqn Ldr. A H Orlebar established a new world speed record of 357.7 mph in 1929 flying the S6, N247. The company pride in its association with high speed flying is evident.

64

65

The final Schneider contest was held at Cowes in September 1931. Shown above is Supermarine's designer at Calshot in August 1931 with a group of Schneider pilots. Left to right: Flt Lt. F W Long, Flt Lt. George Stainforth, Flt Lt. E Hope and Lt. Jerry Brinton RN, killed a few days after the picture was taken as he crashed in N247.

Calshot (below) was the home of the High Speed Flight for both the 1929 and the 1931 contests. This view, taken about 1930, shows the hangars and Henry VIII's castle. The largest hangar was the one that housed the British and Italian teams in 1929 and the Supermarine and Gloster racers in 1931. 44 years after the S5, N220 flew from Calshot as a practice aircraft in the 1931 contest, a replica S5 belonging to Leisure Sport made its maiden flight from Calshot. September 1981, the 50th anniversary of the final contest, will see the replica S5 and some of the original aircraft from Britain, America and Italy come back to Calshot.

66

67

The ultimate development of Mitchell's racing seaplanes came in 1931 thanks to the sponsorship of Lady Houston. Rolls Royce developed a new 'R' engine capable of producing 2,350 hp and Mitchell adapted the S6 design to accommodate it. The overall length was increased and larger floats were produced to provide extra cooling. The resultant S6B's were referred to by their designer as 'flying radiators'. Two were produced, S1595 and S1596. The two existing S6's were modified to the same standard and redesignated S6A's.

Both these photographs show S1595 that won the Schneider Trophy outright on September 13th 1931 with Flt Lt. John Boothman (later Air Chief Marshal) as pilot. The speed was 340 mph. Later the same day S1596 broke the World Air Speed Record at 379 mph, flown by Flt Lt. Stainforth. Two weeks later this was raised by the same pilot to 407.8 mph in S1595. The world speed record for a seaplane was finally established in October 1934 at 440 mph by an Italian Macchi MC72 which holds the record to this day.

Flying to the Empire

Modern air travel has its origins in the formation of the Civil Aerial Transport Committee in 1917. With the end of the great war a number of pioneers established passenger carrying airlines and Southampton's association with flying boat services began in 1919. Hubert Scott-Paine, managing owner of Supermarine Aviation Works Ltd started regular flights from Woolston to Southsea, Bournemouth and the Isle of Wight with Supermarine Channel flying boats, and in August of that year inaugurated the first international service for a short while between Southampton and Le Havre.

1923 saw the formation of the British Marine Air Navigation Company as a joint venture between Supermarine and Southern Railway (who owned Southampton Docks) and regular Friday services were established between Woolston and the Channel Islands and Cherbourg. The fare was £5.50 return. The first flight was undertaken in September 1923 when the flight from the Needles to Cherbourg took 51 minutes. The party on board included Scott-Paine, Sir Sefton Brancker (Director of Civil Aviation) and Capt. H C Biard.

In 1924 the Southampton company was joined with the Handley Page Transport Company and Daimler Airways to form Imperial Airways Ltd. Woolston retained its status as a customs airport for another 10 years and the service to Guernsey continued until 1929. The last year of the service was maintained with Short Calcutta flying boats which were then withdrawn to provide the Mediterranean link on Imperial Airways' India route.

In 1934 the "Empire Air Mail Scheme" which provided for all letters to be carried throughout the Empire without surcharge persuaded Imperial Airways to replace the landplanes on its Empire routes with flying boats. 28 C-Class Empire flying boats were ordered from Shorts of Rochester straight from the drawing board. Southampton was chosen as the centre for the new services, despite serious consideration of Langstone Harbour, Portsmouth, and a maintenance base was established at Hythe in sheds rented from Vickers Supermarine Aviation.

Regular flying boat services were established in March 1937 when the Empire boat Castor arrived at Southampton from Alexandria with 15 passengers on board. Canopus left on the first through service to Durban on 2nd June 1937 and on 29th June the Empire Air Mail Programme was inaugurated to South and East Africa. A few weeks later Caledonia made Imperial Airways' first proving flight across the Atlantic from Hythe to Botwood (Newfoundland) via Foynes on the River Shannon. Cambria also took part and, like Caledonia, had the passenger accommodation reduced to 17 by converting the forward smoking cabin into an extra mail locker. Two tons of mail were now carried. These boats completed five scheduled return trips across the Atlantic during the summer of 1937, and on its last home crossing Cambria made a record crossing over the 2,000 miles from Botwood to Foynes with an average of 190 mph, taking 10 hours, 33 minutes.

The Empire routes were gradually extended as the fleet of 'Empire' boats grew. Karachi was reached in October 1937, Singapore in February 1938, Sydney in the following June and Hong Kong in September 1938. Although 8 flying boats were lost in the first two years, public confidence in them was justified when, for instance, Calypso was forced down in the Channel but was towed by a tug into Cherbourg Harbour.

Facilities for flying boats in Southampton Docks improved and the passing of the Southampton Harbour Act of 1939 confirmed Southampton's status as a marine airport. This gave the Southampton Harbour Board the right to regulate the use of seaplanes and flying boats and a 'reserved area' for aircraft was established off Netley. In September 1938 experiments were carried out in laying a flare path in this area for night flying.

Civilian flying boats continued in service after the outbreak of war in 1939. Indeed, Tasman Empire Airways opened the final leg of the route to Auckland in April 1940. When Italy declared war most of the fleet was transferred to Durban to work on a new 'Horseshoe Route' via East Africa, India and Malaya to Australia, but luxury was sacrificed and the passenger load raised to 29. In 1940 Imperial Airways became part of the British Overseas Airways Corporation (BOAC) and one of the new Corporation's first tasks was to establish a new flying boat base with 400 staff at Poole. Maintenance was, however, retained at Hythe. Several flying boats were commandeered by the RAF, such as the long range Cabot and Caribou, which were lost in the Norway Campaign of 1940.

The invasion of Malaya cut off many boats in Australia and ten were later lost in the war with Japan, but TEAL's Auckland-Sydney run continued with great success until 1947. Clare flew passengers to New York and Clyde surveyed a Poole-Lagos route which was served regularly after October 1940 via Lisbon; Boeing 314 flying boats also flew on this route. Cambria and Coorong were among those which helped evacuate Crete. Cairo was reached via Lagos in July 1941, and in October Empire boats re-established the direct link to Cairo via Gibraltar, flying by night. But the route became too dangerous and was suspended in February 1942, the same month as the Japanese finally cut the India-Australia service.

January 1943 saw six Short Sunderland military flying boats sent back to Rochester to be converted to passenger transports for BOAC, to make up for wartime losses. The type was to supersede the Empire boats and play a major part over the next decade. In August, BOAC received another six conversions and the Poole-Cairo-Karachi service resumed using Sunderlands and West African flights ceased. Another six craft enabled the Karachi-Calcutta link to re-open in May 1944 and later the BOAC fleet of Sunderlands, which they christened the Hythes, reached a maximum of 26. Rangoon was regularly served once more from October 1945, Singapore in January 1946 and Sydney in May.

On 28th November 1945 the first Short Sandringham was launched at Rochester, a fully civilian conversion of the wartime Sunderland, and during 1946 BOAC brought their Hythes up to peacetime airline standards with seats for 22 or 24. This meant the end of the Empire flying boats after a decade's hard work. The class flew 38 million miles in total, but only 13 boats out of 45 survived the war. One of these was offered to the Science Museum in 1947, but sadly it was rejected due to lack of space. Caledonia made the last commercial flight by an Empire boat when she returned to Southampton from South Africa on 12th March 1947, and one survivor lingered at Auckland until the mid-50s, used as a coffee bar!

Although Shorts had in November 1946 launched the first of a new and superior generation of boats to be known as Solent Class, Sandringhams continued to be produced and nine were acquired by BOAC (who called them the Plymouth Class) in January 1947 replacing converted Sunderlands to Sydney and Hong Kong. When three more Sandringhams came early in 1948 they enabled the Hong Kong "Dragon Route" to be extended to Iwakuni, Japan, in March 1948 and on to Tokyo in the following November.

Services returned to Southampton in March 1948 and the latest Solent Class flying boat for BOAC was appropriately christened Southampton by the Mayoress on 14th April, a great day for flying boats which also saw the formal opening of the new air terminal at Berth 50 in the old docks. However, in his speech the Minister of Civil Aviation, Lord Nathan, made it clear that problems lay ahead. Britain alone remained faithful to the big flying boats and her partners on the new Australian services were using faster land planes. The BOAC boats had to carry the full costs of each terminal since there were no other operators to share them.

BOAC were now flying eight boats in and eight out of Southampton each week. There were three Hythes in each direction on the Australia route and one return to Karachi. The Plymouths oper-

ated two services each way weekly, one terminating at Hong Kong and the other at Iwakuni. The Solents flew twice, later three times, weekly each way between Southampton and Vaaldam, near Johannesburg, replacing York land planes.

BOAC's last passenger carrying Hythe boat arrived in Southampton in the afternoon of 16th February 1949. From inaugurating the Australian route in May 1946 to being replaced by Constellations the Hythes had flown 173 million miles and carried 31,000 passengers. Mid-1949 also saw BOAC withdraw their last Plymouths. With them the airline thankfully shed their most expensive marine bases along the Far East route. Flying boat services were then streamlined and 12 of the popular Solents, originally designed for 34 passengers but now able to carry 40, were doing very well on the East and South African services which began to emerge into profit. But instead of increasing services, BOAC cut the projected fleet from 18 to 14 and began to plan service reductions.

Perhaps the reason lay at Hythe where nearly 900 people were needed to maintain this modest fleet. Nevertheless, it came as a shock (not least to management) when on 12th December 1949 BOAC announced that flying boat services from Southampton would be abandoned as soon as a fleet of Hermes land planes was ready.

The final departure for South Africa left Southampton on 3rd November 1950 when the Somerset took off; she returned on Tuesday 14th November flying a twenty-foot laying off pennant and BOAC reached the end of a long and interesting chapter in their history.

However, the use of the marine airport at Southampton was continued by Aquila Airways. The creation of Barry Aikman, DFC, in May 1948, Aquila's first success was on the Berlin airlift. Salt, meat and flour were carried to the beleaguered city, an ideal duty for Aikman's fleet of three ex-BOAC Sunderlands, which made three return trips daily until Lake Havel froze. During the winter Aquila bought another 12

unwanted Sunderlands of the Hythe class at low prices as BOAC took them out of service.

A proving flight by Aquila's Hampshire from Southampton to Madeira on 24th March 1949 was followed in May by a regular weekly service which continued each summer with great success. Aquila also built up a charter business based on flying ships' crews to and from such places as Aden, and holiday-makers' flights between Falmouth and the Scilly Isles began in June 1949.

Aquila received their first Short Solent early in November 1951. This craft took over the Madeira "Sunshine Route" which in 1952 was extended to Las Palmas in the Canaries, leaving Sunderlands on the Madeira-Lisbon shuttle.

Summer routes to the Italian coast were opened in 1954, leaving Southampton every Thursday morning, followed by Genoa and Santa Margherita in 1955. January 1956 saw the newly delivered Solent Aoetearora start a fortnightly direct service from Southampton to Las Palmas and in June 1957 yet another new route, to Montreaux on Lake Geneva opened as part of an inclusive holiday tour.

But this apparent success, based solely on flying boats, suddenly collapsed, as traffic was being taken by charter airlines able to fly direct to a number of holiday resorts from airports such as Luton and Manchester, and there were no replacements available for flying boats. Aquila closed with the last passenger departure by Awateri from Southampton to Madeira on Friday, 26th September 1958, and so ended a remarkable airline, and the end of the boat era.

Supermarine Aviation obtained the first British Certificate of Air Worthiness for a passenger carrying flying boat in August 1919. A cross channel service was inaugurated between Southampton, Le Havre and Cherbourg with this Channel aircraft when a strike paralysed the L & SWR boat services. The venture was short lived and lasted only until 5th October when the strike ended, but was a great success even if one flight to Cherbourg took 5 hours in the teeth of a gale! By the flying boat on the Woolston slipway is Capt. H C Biard, Supermarine's Chief Pilot, and the crowds on the Royal Pier seem more interested in the boat carrying the photographer than the historic event taking place above their heads. Both pictures were taken on the day of the inauguration of the cross channel service.

70

71

The Supermarine Sea Eagle was designed by R J Mitchell for the Channel Island and cross channel service of the British Marine Air Navigation Company formed by Supermarine Aviation and Southern Railway. Six passengers were carried in an enclosed bow cabin with the pilot in an open cockpit in the rear. Three Sea Eagles were built and powered by the Rolls Royce Eagle IX engine of 350 hp. The boats were very popular and remained in service until 1928 when Calcutta flying boats took over the route which was finally abandoned in the following year. Sea Eagle G-EBGS was carefully preserved by Hubert Scott-Paine, and is shown here (below) dwarfed by the Solent Somerset as Victor Scott-Paine presented the old flying boat to BOAC in September 1949. Four years later BOAC broke up the Sea Eagle hull at Heston.

The flying boat **Canopus** (G-ADHL) was prototype of the Short Empire class that inaugurated the Empire Air Mail Scheme in 1937. She was launched and test flown from the Medway on 2nd July 1936, handed over to Imperial Airways on 20th October and entered service ten days later. The photograph of her on the slipway at Rochester shows her roped down as the engines are tested. The Empire or C-Class flying boat was a high wing cantilever monoplane of 114 ft wingspan with an all metal two deck hull.

The lower deck was for passengers and their baggage only. The upper deck housed the crew, mail storage for bedding etc. During the day 24 passengers could be carried with 1½ tons of mail and at night there was sleeping accommodation for 16 passengers. On 22nd October 1936 **Canopus** left on a route proving flight from Southampton to Alexandria via Rome and Brindisi. It was a great triumph. This flying boat logged two million miles before she was withdrawn for scrapping at Hythe in November 1946.

The first Trans-Atlantic proving flights by flying boat were made in July 1937. The first east-west flight was made by Imperial Airways **Caledonia** from the Hythe base via Foynes in Ireland to Botwood, Newfoundland, under Captain A S Wilcockson. The average speed was 132 mph. The flying boat passed an eastbound Pan-Am Sikorsky clipper flying boat making the first American proving flight under Captain Harold E Bray. The Clipper arrived at Hythe at noon on July 8th 1937 to a civic reception led by the Mayor of Southampton and Hubert Scott-Paine. One of these Clippers is seen in this photograph at Hythe with the Empire boat **Courtier** hauled up on the slipway with a beaching chassis for maintenance. Pan-Am used similar flying boats on the Bermuda-New York service which they shared with Imperial Airways.

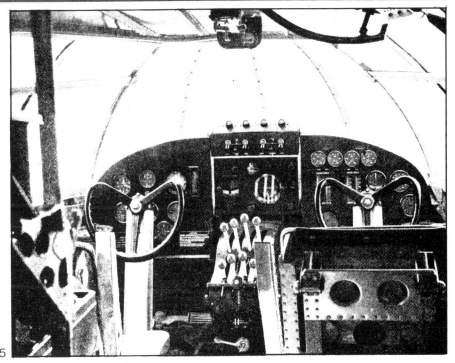

75

The cockpit of an Empire flying boat was considered very spacious and comfortable in 1936. On top of the control panel are the starter and ignition switches of the four engines. Facing the captain and the first officer are instruments for rate-of-climb, air speed, engine revolutions, gyro compass, altimeter and homing indicator. Between the two seats are the four engine throttles and four mixture controls. Behind to starboard there is a hatch through which the navigator could put his head to make his observations.

The provision of reliable high speed launches for the flying boat squadrons of the RAF put the British Power Boat Company of Hythe in the forefront of motor boat production in the 1930s. The owner was Hubert Scott-Paine who as well as being a director of Imperial Airways, was in a position to provide aircraft control tenders to Imperial Airways all over the Empire. The Empire flying boat Centaurus is seen here (above) with a BPBC 37½-ft tender which had accommodation for 20 passengers.

Launches of this sort were supplied to marine air bases as far away as Calcutta, Singapore and South Africa. A "Power" launch is seen in the foreground of the photograph (below) of Centaurus moored off 101 Berth in Southampton Docks with the North German Lloyd liner General von Steuben in 1938.

78

79

Southern Railway provided special trains to connect with the Imperial Airways flying boats at Southampton. At least twice a week the 8.30 left Waterloo with a special portion of two Pullman cars and a brake van with roof boards marked "EMPIRE SERVICE IMPERIAL AIRWAYS". The section was worked into 50 Berth (seen in the photograph above in 1937) and the passengers were transferred to motor launches (below). The flight clerk travelled in the brake van with a desk and weighing machine and compiled the load sheet for a particular flight. Subsequently the service was transferred to Victoria Station close to the Imperial Airways headquarters.

81

Although launches could transport passengers from Hythe it was inconvenient to use moorings established there in December 1936 if the weather was rough. Extra moorings were provided at Marchwood for use in rough weather, but once Imperial Airways had decided against developing Langstone Harbour at Portsmouth in preference to Southampton a special pontoon was installed at Berth 107 in the new docks. This was opened in March 1938 and **Centurion** is seen at the pontoon (above) with Royal Pier in the background. The Red Funnel captains were understandably nervous about flying boats taking off so close to them although they were supposed to land opposite Hythe and taxi in. The photograph (below) gives a delightful impression of the elegance of Empire flying. No doubt the teddy bear travelled free!

82

83

Later in 1938 the flying boat berth was transferred to the far end of the docks at Berth 108. Here a two storey wooden terminal building was erected: it still stands and is fittingly named Imperial House. The photograph (above) shows the flagship **Canopus** and the S23 **Ceres** at the Berth 108 Terminal with **Queen Mary** in the background in the King George V dry dock.

Castor is seen (below) at the Imperial Airways mooring at Hythe. Approaching the flying boat is one of the Imperial Airways flying boat tenders.

CHAMPION

IMPERIAL AIRWAYS
LONDON.

G-·AFCT

989 (b)

84

In 1938 Imperial Airways accepted **Champion** (above) the first of the longer-range S30 Empire flying boats intended for transatlantic-service. In August 1939 the two S30's **Cabot** and **Caribou** began a scheduled nonstop service to Newfoundland re-fuelling in flight over Foynes from a converted Handley Page Harrow bomber. However, only 9 return trips were made on this service before the outbreak of the Second World War.

The first of the even larger G-class, the **Golden Hind** was delivered for trans-Atlantic flights in July 1939. Three were built, **Golden Hind, Golden Fleece** and **Golden Horn** but were taken over by the RAF for long range maritime reconnaissance and special duties. In July 1942 **Hind** and **Horn** were restored to the civilian register and operated from Poole to West Africa via Lisbon. **Horn** crashed at Lisbon in December 1942 but **Hind** survived the war to be luxuriously re-furbished to fly on the Cairo route until it was withdrawn in 1947.

The SHORT "G" CLASS FLYING-BOAT
(four Bristol "Hercules" engines).

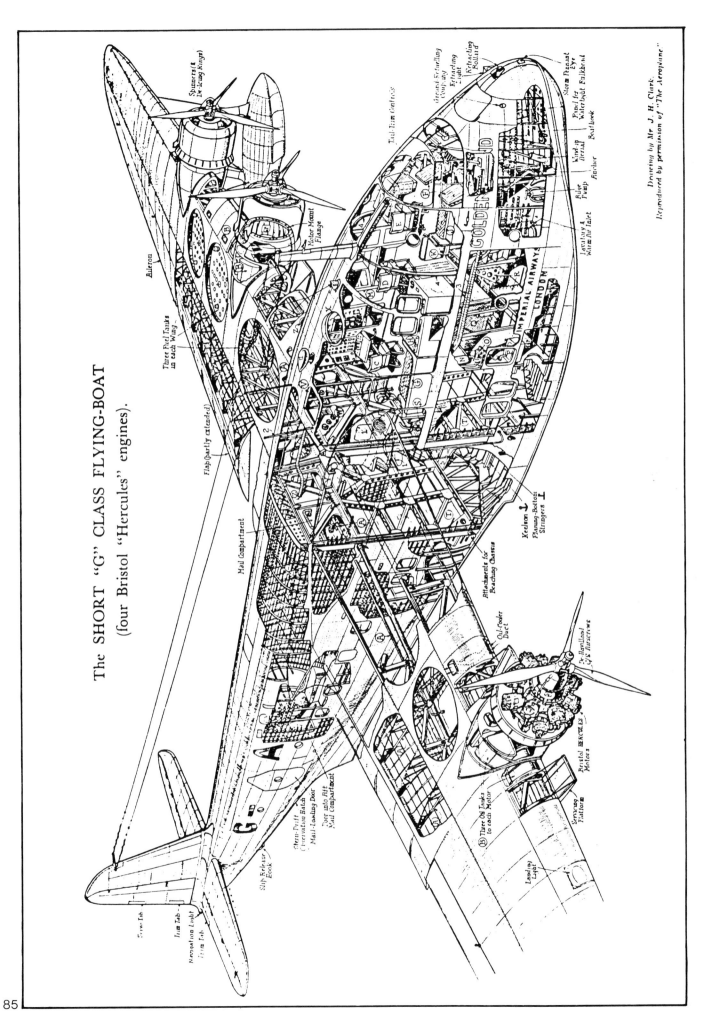

Drawing by Mr J. H. Clark.
Reproduced by permission of "The Aeroplane."

85

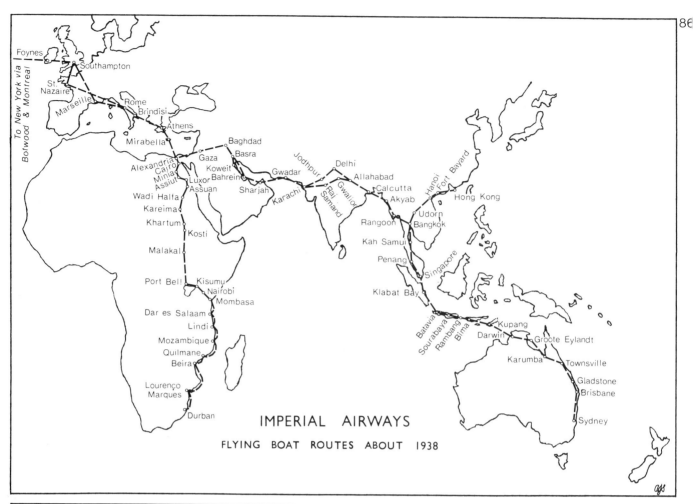

87 Map of routes flown by Imperial Airways.

Advertisement for Imperial Airways 1939.

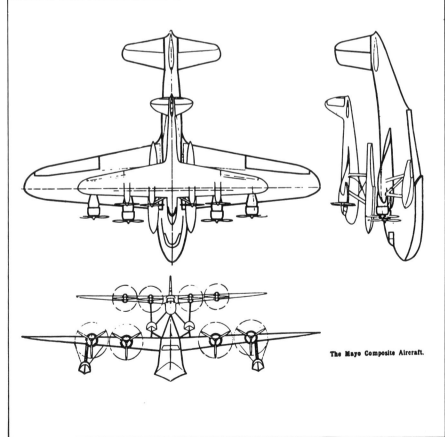

The Mayo Composite Aircraft.

A novel solution to the problem of flying mail across the North Atlantic was found by Imperial Airway's technical advisor, Mr R H Mayo. It was the Mayo Composite Aircraft in which the floatplane **Mercury** was carried on the back of the much larger **Maia**, virtually the same as an Empire flying boat. Not needing the power or fuel to climb from take-off, Mercury could carry 1000 lb of mail for 3,500 miles against a 60 mph wind. The first commercial crossing of the Atlantic was made on 21st July 1938. **Mercury** was launched over Dundee on 6th October 1938 and flew nonstop 6,045 miles to the Orange River in South Africa breaking the world endurance record for seaplanes by a handsome 830 miles.

The photograph shows **Mercury** being lifted onto **Maia's** back by a dockside crane in Southampton on 15th July 1938.

War time losses to the BOAC fleet were made good by transferring RAF Sunderland aircraft to the civil register. The flying boats were converted for passenger carrying and named the Hythe class by BOAC. In all 26 Hythes such as G-AGER seen here in war time drab were acquired. In August 1943 the flying boats resumed the Poole-Cairo-Karachi service and in May 1944 the Karachi-Calcutta link was re-opened. Rangoon was served regularly from October 1945, Singapore in January 1946 and Sydney in May 1946. The photograph (below) shows a war time Hythe class undergoing maintenance at Hythe.

92

93

On 28th November 1945 the first Short Sandringham was launched at Rochester — a fully civilian version of the wartime Sunderland and in November 1946 Short's launched the first of a new and superior flying boat, the Solent class intended for the Far East and the East Africa route. The photograph shows the Short Solent Scapa in 1948 over the Hythe base. After conversion to a Solent 3 in 1950 this boat flew as City of York. On 14th April 1948 the Mayoress of Southampton christened the latest Solent flying boat Southampton at the inauguration of a new marine air terminal at Berth 50 in the Old Docks. The ceremony was performed using an antique silver ewer filled with Empire wine. But despite the optimism of the day words of warning were uttered by the Minister of Civil Aviation, Lord Nathan, who asked in his speech whether "passengers would choose the more speedy land planes or the more roomy flying boats".

94

95

The end of BOAC's flying boat services on 3rd November 1950 was sudden and unexpected. The photograph shows management and staff waving goodbye to Somerset as she leaves for South Africa. It was the last BOAC passenger departure from Southampton although a mere six months earlier a proposed administrative re-organisation of BOAC had envisaged a flying boat base remaining at Hythe. At the same time, with a sense of history BOAC named their new Boeing Stratocruisers after the old C-Class Empire flying boats.

Extracts from the flight logs of Flt Lt. G A Kirkwood DFM. They were made in 1950 near the end of BOAC's time with Solent's on the Southampton-Vaaldam (Johannesburg) run and record flights with Somerset, City of York (ex Scapa), City of London and City of Cardiff.

RECORD OF FLIGHTS.

Date.	Aircraft.		Engines.		Journey.		Time of Departure.		Time of Arrival.		Time in Air.	
	Type.	Markings.	Type.	H.P.	From.	To.	Hrs.	Mins.	Hrs.	Mins.	Hrs.	Mins.
						Brought forward	...	...	...	...	449	11 44
20·9·50	"	G·AHIO	"	"	S'hampton	Augusta	06	32	13	12	6	40
20·9·50	"	"	"	"	Augusta	Alexandria	14	24	19	24	5	00
21·9·50	"	G·AHIS	"	"	Alexandria	Augusta	12	46	18	39	5	53
22·9·50	"	"	"	"	Augusta	Biscarosse	04	05	10	23	6	18
22·9·50	"	"	"	"	Biscarosse	S'hampton	12	18	15	24	3	06
26·9·50	"	G·AKNO	"	"	S'hampton	Augusta	10	37	18	00	7	23
27·9·50	"	"	"	"	Augusta	Alexandria	05	31	10	48	5	25
27·9·50	"	"	"	"	Alexandria	Luxor	12	16	14	43	2	27
28·9·50	"	G·AKNO	"	"	Luxor	Khartoum	03	24	07	17	3	53
28·9·50	"	"	"	"	Khartoum	Port Bell	08	16	14	22	6	06
29·9·50	"	"	"	"	Port Bell	Victoria Falls	04	50	12	03	7	13
30·9·50	"	"	"	"	Victoria Falls	Vaaldam	06	25	09	50	3	25
5·10·50	"	G·AKNP	"	"	Vaaldam	Victoria Falls	09	26	13	05	3	39
6·10·50	"	"	"	"	Victoria Falls	C'maclear	03	53	08	33	4	40
6·10·50	"	"	"	"	C'maclear	Port Bell	09	26	14	50	5	24
7·10·50	"	"	"	"	Port Bell	Khartoum	03	44	09	50	6	12
						Carried forward	...	...	...	...	494	38

96

97

Aquila Airways carried out a proving flight from Southampton to Madeira in their ex-BOAC Hythe class Sunderland named **Hampshire**. Above she is seen taxi-ing between Town Quay and the terminal at Berth 50, in 1949 and below she is seen at Madeira. **Hampshire** was one of the aircraft used by Aquila in the Berlin airlift, and in January 1950 was put at the disposal of Winston Churchill who was on holiday at Funchal Bay and who had to dash back for the General Election.

98

99

In June 1950 Aquila Airways tried to establish a service from Southampton to Edinburgh and Glasgow. The first (and only) departure is seen here with a Hythe flying boat taking off with a Union Castle liner in the background. The route failed as there were insufficient bookings to make it profitable. However, Aquila did establish a successful Southampton — Jersey service on 7th July 1950, twice every summer Saturday until the end of the 1951 season.

Aquila's maintenance was done by Air Service Training at Hamble using the slipway originally built for A V Roe about 1916. The maintenance base is seen here in 1955 with both Solent and Hythe flying boats in evidence.

a

b

101 (a, b, & c)

c

Aquila Airways received their first Solent flying boats early in November 1955. The degree of comfort available in these aircraft is clear from the drawing of Aoetearora II acquired by the airline from Tasman Empire Airways in 1955. The boat could carry about 40 passengers and a crew of seven in its two decks. There was comfortable seating for passengers, a promenade, a bar, a dining room, and even a ship's library. In the days of BOAC if not Aquila, the food was excellent and served on real crockery. Luxury of this sort is unknown to the modern traveller even though he can now travel at twice the speed of sound.

In 1955 Aquila Airways purchased three Short Solent 4 flying boats from Tasman Empire Airways. The first to arrive was RMA **Awateri** shown here (above) arriving at Southampton after an 8-day journey from Darwin — still in Tasman Empire Airways livery. On arrival she was overhauled at the Hamble Maintenance base. The following January **Awateri** inaugurated a direct Southampton — Las Palmas service. **Aoete-arora II** (Maori for 'Land of the Long White Cloud') is seen (below) arriving from Darwin on 18th May 1955. The flying boat had been named at Belfast in May 1949 by the then Princess Elizabeth and it carried her as Queen with Prince Philip on their tour of New Zealand in 1953.

The inherent safety of flying boats was again confirmed when Aquila Airways **Hungerford** bound for Madeira crashed while taking off on 28th January 1953. There were no casualties but the flying boat sank while being towed towards Calshot. She sank in the mud between Fawley Pier and the RAF Station and is seen here upside down in the water. Near the camera is the starboard wing float and beyond is the tail of the aircraft.

However, disaster struck when on 15th November 1957 the Solent **Sydney** crashed into a chalk pit near Chessel on the Isle of Wight after taking off from Southampton for Lisbon. There was a loss of 35 lives but 15 survived the crash. The disaster hastened the end of Aquila Airways.

106

**Southampton Harbour Board
Proposed Airport – Southampton Water
Master Plan of Development, Scheme 2**

107

Awateri at the marine air terminal at Berth 50 on 26th September 1958. When she left for Madeira later that day she became the last passenger carrying flying boat to leave Southampton. She returned the following Tuesday and at 0900 hours on 20th December 1958 the last of the three Solents remaining at Southampton, left for Lisbon where plans were laid for a new service to Madeira. But the three flying boats lay idle on the River Tagus for 13 years before being broken up.

A scheme for a combined sea and land airport on the east side of Southampton Water was published by the Southampton Harbour Board in December 1943. Situated between the Hamble and Meon rivers, the airport would have had a railway link at Southwick. After the war the scheme was considered by the Ministry of Civil Aviation in competition with similar schemes for Langstone Harbour, Portsmouth and for Cliffe near Gravesend. There was also a proposal to build two water runways on the north side of Heathrow Airport. In the event none of the projects were undertaken.

108

109

At the end of the war it was decided that the UK-New York route would best be served by flying boats. In December 1945 Saunders-Roe of Cowes began design work on a giant flying boat based on their A37 design of 1939. Designated the SR45 it was a 140 ton craft taking 100 passengers with a cruising speed of 370 mph and a range of 5,000 miles. Three aircraft were ordered for BOAC by the Ministries of Supply and Civil Aviation and the name "Princess" was adopted. The aircraft were powered by ten Bristol Proteus 600 propeller-turbine engines but they were still underpowered. The cost to the taxpayer rose from the estimated £2.8 million to £10 million by 1950 and the project would have been scrapped had it not been for the interest shown by British South American Airlines. The picture (above) shows the massive hull of the flying boat taking shape at Saunders-Roe in 1949 while (below) a complete fuselage with stub wings is towed out of the Cowes factory in 1951.

It was still hoped to fly the Princess to Buenos Aires in 1953. One boat was launched in August 1952 and eventually flew, a hugely impressive aircraft by the standards of the day, "running high and proud in the Solent like an ocean liner with wings, spearheading a giant cloud of spray". The other two boats were cocooned unfinished at Cowes while G-ALUM (above) remained on the slip at Columbine Works, Cowes.

A Bahamas-based company bought all three aircraft intending to convert them for land use and began chopping off the bits they wanted. However, eventually the Calshot boats were scrapped and the only completed Princess (below) was towed slowly up the River Itchen for demolition. The Supermarine slipway from which the first flying boat services had left 47 years earlier was considered as a site for the demolition but times had changed and it was clearly not strong enough for these giant aircraft.

112   113

In July 1937, Vicker's Supermarine presented the S6A N248 to Southampton Corporation in whose borough the Trophy winning seaplanes were built. During the Second World War the aircraft was featured in the film **First of the Few** and at the Denham film studios it was repainted to represent S1595 the S6B that established a new world speed record in 1931. For years the aircraft was stored in a hangar at the Borough Airport at Eastleigh until it was displayed at Royal Pier masquerading under its false colours. Here it suffered badly from corrosion and eventually it was displayed in the RJ Mitchell Museum opened by private initiative in 1976 (above). In 1981 the future of the Museum and the aircraft is in doubt. Other aircraft are preserved in museums up and down the country. The Supermarine S6B S1596 is in the Science Museum, and a Supermarine Walrus is in the Hendon RAF Museum (below).

114

115

Only three survivors are known from the 110 or so big flying boats built for BOAC and other airlines between 1936 and the late 1940's. One of the three Solents bought by Howard Hughes is still at San Francisco. An ex-Royal New Zealand Air Force Sunderland is now in the Virgin Islands and may shortly return to this country. The third boat is the Sandringham **Southern Cross**. The flying boat was bought by Tasman Empire Airways as **Auckland** and in 1949 was sold to Barrier Reef Airways of Brisbane and after 22 years passed to Antilles Air Boats Inc of the US Virgin Islands when it was given its present name. **Southern Cross** is seen (above) in Antilles livery when it visited the Solent in 1977. She has now been acquired by a group of enthusiasts who flew her to the Solent from Puerto Rico in 1981 and it is now undergoing restoration at Calshot (below).

Let us hope that it will be found a suitable permanent home.

Imperial Airways and BOAC — Fleet List

Short S23 C-Class Empire Flying Boats

G-ADHL	Canopus	G-ADHM	Caledonia	G-ADUT	Centaurus
G-ADUU	Cavalier	G-ADUV	Cambria	G-ADUW	Castor
G-ADUX	Cassiopeia	G-ADUY	Capella	G-ADUZ	Cygnus
G-ADVA	Capricornus	G-ADVB	Corsair	G-ADVC	Courtier
G-ADVD	Challenger	G-ADVE	Centurion	G-AETV	Coriolanus
G-AETW	Calpurnia	G-AETX	Ceres	G-AETY	Clio
G-AETZ	Circe	G-AEUA	Calypso	G-AEUB	Camilla
G-AEUC	Corinna	G-AEUD	Cordelia	G-AEUE	Cameronian
G-AEUF	Corinthian	G-AEUG	Coogee	G-AEUH	Corio
G-AEUI	Coorong	G-AFBK	Coolangatta	G-AEBL	Cooee

Short S26 G-Class Flying Boats

G-AFCI	Golden Hind	G-AFCS	Golden Fleece	G-AFCK	Golden Horn

Short S30 and S33 C-Class Empire Flying Boats

G-AFCT	Champion	G-AFCU	Cabot	G-AFCV	Caribou
G-AFCW	Connemara	G-AFCX	Clyde	G-AFCY	Awarua
C-AFCZ	Australia (Clare)	G-AFDA	Aoetearora	G-AFKZ	Cathay
G-AFPZ	Clifton	G-AFRA	Cleopatra		

Short S25 Sunderland "Hythe" Class Flying Boats

G-AGER	Hadfield	G-AGEU	Hampshire	G-AGEV	Hailsham
G-AGEW	Hanwell	G-AGHV	Hamble	G-AGHW	Hamilton
G-AGHX	Harlequin	G-AGHZ	Hawkesbury	G-AGIA	Haslemere
G-AGIJ	Henley	G-AGJK	Howard	G-AGJL	Hobart
G-AGJM	Hythe	G-AGJN	Hudson	G-AGJO	Honduras
G-AGKV	Huntingdon	G-AGKW	Hotspur	G-AGKX	Himalaya
G-AGKY	Hungerford	G-ACKZ	Harwich	G-AGLA	Hunter
G-AHEO	Halstead	G-AHEP	Hanbury	G-AHER	Helmsdale

Also three un-named boats G-AGES, G-AGET and G-AGIB.

Shorts S25 Sandringham "Plymouth" Class Flying Boats

G-AHZA	Penzance	G-AHYY	Portsmouth	G-AHZB	Portland
G-AGZC	Pembroke	G-AHZD	Portmarnock	G-AHZE	Portsea
G-AHZF	Poole	G-AHZG	Pevensey	G-AJMZ	Perth
G-AKCR	St Andrew	G-AKCO	St George	G-AKOP	St David

Short S45 Solent Flying Boats

G-AHIL	Salisbury	G-AHIM	Scarborough	G-AHIN	Southampton (City of Southampton)
A-AHIO	Somerset (City of Edinburgh)	G-AHIR	Sark	G-AHIS	Scapa (City of York)
G-AHIT	Severn	G-AHIU	Solway		
G-AHIW	Stornaway	G-AHIX	Sussex	G-AHIV	Salcombe
G-AKNO	City of London	G-AKNP	City of Cardiff	G-AHIY	Southsea
G-AKNS	City of Liverpool			G-AKNR	City of Belfast

Short Mayo Composite Aircraft

G-ADHK	Maia	G-ADHJ	Mercury

Aquila Airways Ltd

Short S25 Sunderland Flying Boats

G-AGER	Hadfield
G-AGEU	Hampshire
G-AGHZ	Hawkesbury
G-AGIA	Hazlemere
G-AGJJ	Henley
G-AGJK	Howard
G-AGJL	Hobart
G-AGJM	Hythe
G-AGJN	Hudson
G-AGKY	Hungerford
G-AGLA	Hudson
G-AHEO	Halstead
G-AHER	Helmsdale

Short S25 Sandringham Flying Boat

G-AGKX	Himalaya

Short S45 Solent Flying Boats

G-AHIN	Southampton
G-AKNU	Sydney
G-ANAJ	City of Funchal
G-ANYI	Awateri
G-AOBL	Aeotearora

Photograph Acknowledgements

Charles Bowyer   1
British Airways   81, 82, 92, 93
British Transport Docks Board   88
Beken of Cowes   50
Flight International   59, 67, 72, 73, 75, 83, 85
M H Goodall   7, 14, 15, 16, 17, 18, 45
Janes Aircraft   89
G A Kirkwood   95
R J Mitchell Museum   11, 12, 13, 27, 29, 30, 31, 32, 35, 36, 37, 38, 39, 48, 52, 54, 55, 58, 61, 62, 64, 65
R A F Museum, Hendon   40, 113
Short Bros. & Harland   84, 100, 101
Nigel Smith   86, 107
John Scott-Paine   43
Science Museum   3, 5, 6, 41, 44
Southampton City Record Office   77, 80
Southampton City Museums   2, 4, 8, 19, 20, 21, 22, 23, 24, 25, 26, 28, 33, 34, 46, 47, 49, 51, 53, 56, 57, 60, 63, 66, 68, 69, 70, 76, 87
Southampton University Industrial Archaeology Group   42
Southern Newspapers Ltd.   10, 71, 78, 79, 83, 94, 96, 97, 98, 99, 102, 103, 104, 105, 106, 108, 109, 111, 112, 114, 115
Saunders-Roe   110
Steve Wolf   89, 90
Bill White   9, 74

Acknowledgements

The Editor and contributors would like to thank the Officers and the Editorial Committee of the Southampton University Industrial Archaeology Group for all their help and encouragement. In addition special mention should be made of the following:

Les Smith, British Transport Docks Board

Miss Sheila Thomson, Southampton Record Office

Robert Burrell, Southampton Reference Library

Peter Ashton, Librarian, Southern Evening Echo

R A Wardale, Editor, Southern Evening Echo

Sqn Ldr. Alan Jones, R J Mitchell Museum

Steve Wolf, Dept. of Aeronautics, Southampton University

British Airways

Mr & Mrs J Ridgeway

Designed by A W Williams